Presented to:

_____

From:

_____

Date:

_____

A BOOK OF HOPE

for Mothers

CELEBRATE THE JOY OF CHILDREN

written by ... Heather Hurd   *edited by* ... Kathy Knight & Cecil O. Kemp, Jr.

written by ...
Heather Hurd

A very, very special thanks to ...
Stephen von Hagel, Robert Kiefer and Brenda McClearen. Stephen had the idea for The Hope Collection and shepherded the creative effort, working closely with Robert, Brenda and their associates.

edited by ...
Kathy Knight and Cecil O. Kemp, Jr.

Art Direction ...
McClearen Design Studios
3901 Brush Hill Rd.   Nashville, TN 37216   615-859-4550

To Reach the Author and Publisher ...
The Wisdom Company, Inc.
P. O. Box 681351   Franklin, TN 37068-1351
1-615-791-7186

About The Hope Collection –

Each Hope Collection book is based on Cecil O. Kemp, Jr's acclaimed inspirational book, **Wisdom Honor & Hope**.

Hope—without it, no one can live very long.

No great conquests have ever been won without it.

No one has ever seen better days without hoping for them.

Nurture hope and it will reward you.

Hope is the sunshine of life and the angel that puts a song in your heart.

What gives you hope?

The authors and publishers invite you to enjoy this and other Hope Collection Gift Books.

About the Creator of The Hope Collection –

Cecil O. Kemp, Jr. lived his dream, becoming a successful businessman and business owner. Yet, he was very unfulfilled. Enormous material success didn't deliver on its promises of hope and happiness. He set out to discover the secrets of a genuinely happy, hopeful life. Finding and applying them, he freed himself and his family from the rat race life, while enjoying even greater material success. After nearly two decades of this higher prosperity, he offers those amazing discoveries in The Hope Collection. Kemp and other Hope Collection writers invite readers to begin their own journey of the heart toward real and lasting peace, hope, happiness and success.

Introduction

Motherhood. Let's face it—for most of us, this word means frustration mixed with smiles, the loss of personal space and time, battles of individual (and determined) wills, the difficult balancing act of work and family.

How refreshing, then, to read Heather Hurd's loving and wisdom-filled thoughts on this very important job of Motherhood. She reminds us all (and we certainly do need reminding!) that the mother is the spiritual core of the home—which means a lot of hard work yet also wondrous amazement, joy and a heart of gratitude for the job given to us.

Thank you, Heather, for confirming (with your beautiful "new-mother" enthusiasm) that ours is a divine task that places us in the very midst of creation and spiritual responsibility. This may not ease the stress of our busy lives, but it certainly beats any job description I know of!

Tonight I plan on kneeling with my daughter to pray.
–Kathryn Knight, editor

Dedication

The book is dedicated to my mother, Patty Kemp.

You help me to see the preciousness of life found in my children. If they ever know deep motherly love as have Rusty and I, they will be blessed. Thank you for being dedicated to making an eternal difference in this world by following the path of Wisdom, Honor & Hope. As it is described in Proverbs, you are truly a woman of noble character, a personification of wisdom.
–Heather Hurd, author

Acknowledgement

This book is also written in wonderful memory of Ashley Fly.

Children

*Children are the living messages
we send to a time we will not see.*
— Neil Postman

*Houses are made of brick
and mortar; a home is built
of love, because its heart is
a mother.*
— Cecil O. Kemp, Jr.

How we raise our children, what we
teach them through example, and the
manner in which we express our
feelings to them will leave impressions
on this world forever.

Through our children, we can make a difference in a world that seems to be crumbling at every turn. Our children can embody real Hope for a world torn by hatred, anger, greed, deception, lust, and evil. All the ills of this world cannot be blamed on bad parenting. And yet much of the good in this world is the result of parents' spending time with their children, teaching them by example, and showing them that they love them.

Anything we dream for our children and families is possible.

We choose which seeds we will plant in the lives of our children: good or evil; kindness or rudeness; selflessness or selfishness; happiness or sorrow; love or hatred; life or death. One day, those seeds will come to fruition, whether or not we live to see the harvest.

The mother who wants to assure a legacy of excellence and lasting success shows her heart to be full of unconditional love and walks the path of Wisdom, Honor, and Hope.

🌐 Nugget of Hope
Living models of Eternal Truth reveal God to our children, molding their hearts and minds so they can be Shining Stars lighting up their world with hope, kindness, honor, dependability, and love.
—Cecil O. Kemp, Jr.

Landmarks

*Lives of great people remind us we
can make our lives sublime and leave behind us*

—Robert Longfellow

Every life has landmarks. My dad says landmarks are the turning points in our lives that teach us and change us.

Mothers' landmarks remain in their children's memories; no one can erase them. They mark the birthplace of wise and unwise habits in a child's life.

When I was a small child, my mother would take my brother and me to the airport to pick up our dad. I remember so well running to the gate, looking expectantly for Dad's plane to land, and being so excited when he stepped off the plane. Mother felt that way, too, and knew that was how we felt. That's why she loaded up two wild kids in the car, bravely taking them to the airport late at night—to demonstrate to us the importance she placed on welcoming our dad home at the end of a long business trip. Those were frequent occasions back then that remain wonderful memories today. Our mother's thoughtfulness toward our dad created inner spiritual footprints and impressions—landmarks—that will always be with us.

As mothers, we set personal examples that become landmarks in the memories of our children.

Nugget of Hope

Wise examples by mothers create in their children inner landmarks of wisdom, honor, and hope.

Responsibility

Some things you can count,
do not really count.

Some things you cannot count,
really do count.

—*Albert Einstein*

Parents typically pay their children an allowance to perform household or other tasks. This practice certainly has its merits; for example, earning and spending an allowance can teach children how to handle money wisely. An allowance can be a particularly good teaching tool for a child who has reached the age when more "adult-like" tasks can be assigned. By that time, children should be mentally and emotionally mature enough to truly understand the importance of financial responsibility and accountability.

But these early learning opportunities can teach far more important lessons. Tasks such as making beds, putting clothes in their proper place, and taking trash to the curb serve our children better, in the long run, if we use them to teach true responsibility and accountability, without waving financial "carrots." Why? Because our children need to learn that everything they do, or do not do, will have consequences and that being responsible pays the best rewards.

The principles of Wisdom give us, as parents, the responsibility for teaching our children about values. Wise parents take joy in teaching their children to serve others and to do their best, without harming another person or seeking financial reward.

🌐 Nugget of Hope

Knowing you have done your best and served others is better than any financial reward.

Habit

Sow acts, reap habits; sow habits,
reap a character; sow a character,
reap a destiny.
—George Boardman

To achieve excellence and true success in life, mothers and their children need to concentrate their hearts and minds on what is truly important. Mothers can teach their children wise habits that will help them develop sound character—the basis of wise choices that determine destiny, in this life and for eternity.

Children like habit because predictability seems normal and comfortable to them. It is our responsibility as mothers to develop wise habits, since our children will see and adopt our models. For example, many mothers get into the wise habit of setting a child's bath for a certain time each night. They compound their wisdom, and teach the child wise habits, by having the child pick out a book for a bedtime story. Then, the mother and child read the story. Next, they turn out the lights and kneel together to pray beside the child's bed. After a few nights of this routine, the child will protest if the mother skips a step! This child will likely carry these habits into adulthood and parenting.

Children and teenagers, like adults, develop habits that lead them where they most desire to go. Our children learn values and priorities for life from our habits.

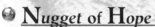

● **Nugget of Hope**

Wise habits are the means by which our wise inner spirit person carries us to freedom and security.

Time

Teach us to number our days, realize how few they are, and spend them wisely.

-King David

Our life is currency we spend only once.

—Cecil O. Kemp, Jr.

A new mother can convince anyone of the importance of spending time with loved ones and friends.

Before our son was born, I could not imagine being away from work longer than four weeks. The idea of being a stay-at-home mother, giving up my career, income, and status as a professional financial planner, blew my mind.

Then, along came the J-man—our beautiful son, Justus! I was overwhelmed with unconditional love. Suddenly, I realized the importance for us of being with our son, as much as possible and especially in his formative years. We would never be able to earn enough money or status to buy back that precious time with Justus. Every time he smiles that wonderful "I've got you wrapped around my pinkie" smile, I thank God for giving us wisdom from above to see the importance of spending every second we can with Justus.

As mothers, none of us want to look back in regret that we did not take our children to the playground, kiss them, hold them, and put them to bed. The time we spend with our children when they are young is irreplaceable—for them and for us.

● Nugget of Hope

Material possessions, education, and status can never replace the wisdom and beautiful memories gained by spending time with those we love.

Passion

*Where your
treasure is,
there will
your heart
be also.*

—*Jesus*

It is impossible to fool our hearts. Our treasures
(passions) live in our hearts and, thus,
are inseparable from who we are. Whatever we
treasure most in life is what we will most certainly

throw our total being into. Our treasures are the things we hold most dear—beauty beyond description.

Do your treasures consist of career, fancy cars, bank or investment accounts, or intellectual pursuits? Or is the passion of your life serving God by serving others, especially your children?

Once, material things were my treasures. However, they never brought me (or anyone else) the true happiness, satisfaction, and joy for which we long. I found those when I chose to treasure deeply my personal, harmonious, spiritual relationship with God. The inner spiritual peace from that relationship ignited in me the passion that sees the treasure of relationships with my children, family, friends, and associates.

Wise mothers provide personal examples and nurture only those passions in their children that will have durable and eternally lasting value. Once you find your treasures, there will be no limit to what you will do to keep them.

Nugget of Hope

What we value most becomes the passion of our life.

Concentration

Singleness of purpose is one of the chief essentials for success in life, no matter what may be one's aim.

—John D. Rockefeller, Jr.

Concentration is the act of focusing the inner person upon a given goal, until ways and means for realizing that goal have been developed and successfully put into habitual operation.

Isn't it amazing what we can accomplish in just a single day when we set our minds to it? With the phone ringing, errands to run, ballgames, a home to care for, a family to tend to, giving your time to your employer—it really takes concentration to get things accomplished!

Ideally, a mother's schedule will be flexible enough to be quickly changed, should unscheduled matters involving our children or family need our attention.

The greatest values of concentration are these: first, concentration assures we focus on what is truly important; second, concentration means we are able to lie down to sleep each night knowing that our day's activities accomplished a great deal of good.

Nugget of Hope
Concentration on important purpose
is the key to truly lasting success.

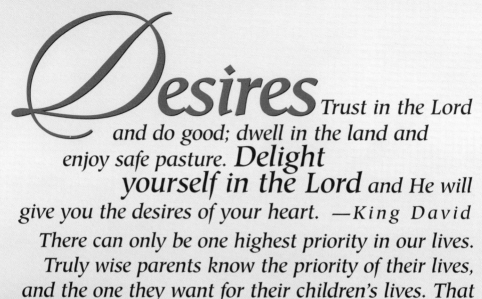

Desires

Trust in the Lord and do good; dwell in the land and enjoy safe pasture. **Delight yourself in the Lord** *and He will give you the desires of your heart.* —King David

There can only be one highest priority in our lives. Truly wise parents know the priority of their lives, and the one they want for their children's lives. That should be achieving and maintaining inner spiritual peace.
—Cecil O. Kemp, Jr.

The desires that I have for my husband, Chris, and our son, Justus, are great and profound. My deepest inner hopes for The J-man are not financial, intellectual, or physical in nature, although I hope he has those gifts.

Every night as I put him to bed I pray: "Lord, watch over him tonight; keep him from sickness and death. Make Justus' life usable for You. I pray that You would use every part of him to make a difference in this world for your Kingdom. Use his mind, his eyes, his lips, his tongue, his hands, his feet—every part of him for your glory. Make him a mighty spiritual warrior for You! God, I pray that he would come to know You as his Lord and Savior at a very young age and proclaim your name all the days of his life. I pray that You would grant unto him long life. Let him know how much his daddy and I love him, his grandparents, aunts, uncles, and cousins love him. Most of all let him know how much You love him. Keep him, I pray."

These are the deepest inner desires of my heart—a mother's heart.

Nugget of Hope

Hold wise desires in your heart, for your children, family, and all others.

Self-Control

Be swift to hear, slow to speak,
slow to wrath. —St. James
As much as it is within your control, live
peaceably with everyone. —St. Paul

Unwillingness to exercise self-control, Wisdom's way, is the single greatest cause of broken relationships.

Think about the quotations above. They tell us exactly what self-control means. We are not born with self-control! That is why we need a supernatural boost from God's self-control inside us, through the influence of the Spirit of God. Even then, self-control, Wisdom's way, must be practiced. It is often difficult to practice self-control.

Perhaps that is what makes it so significant.

As mothers, we have a tremendous impact on our children when we do (and do not) practice self-control in everyday living and working. Self-control, Wisdom's way, is one of the most important behavior models a mother gives her children.

Nugget of Hope
Self-control is a conscious choice to control self-attention.

Forgiveness

Life is a circle. **The seeds we sow become the harvest we reap.**

—Cecil O. Kemp, Jr.

Really forgiving is forgetting what you forgave. **Mercy and grace** *will be shown to you as you show these to others.*

—St. Paul

Wisdom instructs that forgiveness is a choice, so we should not just forgive if and when we feel like it. A mother who makes the biggest difference in her family's and children's lives is moved by unconditional love. She forgives first and truly forgets what has been forgiven. Wisdom instructs us to deal with our attitudes by forgiving others completely, regardless of what they may have said or done.

In mother-daughter relationships, the potential for conflict escalates as the daughter begins her teenage years. I dated the same young man from age fifteen until I married him at age twenty. My mother encouraged me to date others and was not exactly thrilled when I announced that Chris and I were engaged. I was hurt by her reaction when I showed her my engagement ring. That I can laugh about it now is proof of the power of forgiveness. Mother asked me to forgive her, and I did.

My mother and my husband now get along wonderfully. This special blessing will help my children to grow up in a family where harmony and unity prevail.

Forgiveness is Wisdom's first step to ending conflicts and beginning the healing process.

⬤ **Nugget of Hope**

True forgiveness heals, restores, and assures unity and harmony.

Choice

Our life is the sum of our choices, the direct result of acting on our beliefs. Our life is a self-portrait of these: the philosophy and habits we choose for daily living and working. —Cecil O. Kemp, Jr.

The greatest human power is our God-given right of total freedom to make our own choices. When we live wisely and work according to the Philosophy of Wisdom and the principles of Wisdom, we make wise choices which stand the test of time.

As mothers, we have the choice and the opportunity to make a positive or negative difference in this world, especially through the influence of our lives on our children. Our children learn by example. We set before them an example with every choice we make.

Thus, we play an immeasurable role in our children's lives.

We choose what our influence will be. We make the choice of running our lives in overdrive, preoccupied with the unimportant. Or, we can spend more of our time with our children, doing things with them such as playing ball, having a tea party, swimming, riding bikes, reading books, or just sitting together sharing "hang time"! The choice of activity is less important than the choice to spend time together.

Our choosing to spend time with our children will make a big difference in our lives—and theirs.

● **N**ugget of **H**ope
Destiny is the consequence of choice, not chance.

Influence

No one is a light **unto themselves,** *not even the sun.*

—*Antonio Porchia*

Our example removes any doubt about our theories.   —*Cecil O. Kemp, Jr.*

What we do is what influences our children most. As mothers, we definitely have a sphere of influence, especially in the home, where we take a leadership role. Through our personal conduct, we demonstrate what is expected of others within our environment.

Let's pretend for a moment that you are a skilled writer with the ability to inspire others. You write the award-winning speech of the year. That's wonderful, but this fact remains: no matter how wonderful your speech or story, the example you set is still what will most influence all in your sphere of influence.

Consider the truth contained in the old saying, "Actions speak louder than words." That's what influence is all about. We choose whether our influence will be positive or negative. That is determined largely by the philosophy of life and the habits by which we choose to live and work.

We have the opportunity through the influence of our personal example to make a great and positive difference in the lives of others, especially our children.

Nugget of **Hope**
The influence of our beliefs, principles, and values is greatest in our personal example.

Praise

The deepest priciple

*The deepest principle in human nature is the **craving to be appreciated**.*

—William James

To say, "well done" to any bit of good work is to take hold of the powers which have made the effort and strengthen them beyond our knowledge!—Phillips Brooks

Everyone has the desire to be appreciated and praised! Wise people are always aware of this. They make it their life's business always to show their appreciation for others. Often, a little bit of praise and encouragement is all that someone needs to reach a goal. Few things in this world are more powerful and lasting than a word of encouragement or sincere praise.

Praise can uplift someone. It can be that extra "push" that is needed to make it through the task at hand and can cause someone to achieve greater results.

My dad often talks about his great aunt, Gillie McKinley. I found this story from his book *Wisdom Honor & Hope* to be especially valuable for me, as a mother.

Dad says Aunt Gillie was very influential in his life, like a second mother to him. Aunt Gillie's words were always uplifting. The Wisdom and Honor she possessed allowed her to impart Hope to my dad. Her words of encouragement made him feel ten feet tall and inspired him to dream big dreams. Aunt Gillie saw great possibilities in my father's small accomplishments. She took the time to compliment him and to show that faithfulness in little things led to achieving big dreams.

human nature is the craving to be appreciated

Nugget of Hope

Help your children feel good about themselves. Kind words and praise cost nothing and accomplish much.

Strength

I have never been one who thought the Lord should make life easy; I've just asked Him to make me strong.   —Eva Bowring

Out of the lowest depths there is a path to the loftiest height.   —Elbert Hubbard

Most of us tend to need the most strength in times of crisis or tragedy. Typically, we respond in one of three ways:

- we become emotionally and spiritually numb from denial;

- we allow trauma to destroy us and affect others we influence; or

- we use crisis and tragedy as seeds for growth and greater success in our lives.

Inner strength can fortify your emotions and see you through the most difficult of times. We are not promised a life without sorrow, pain, or hardship. When troubles abound, we can endure if we have a harmonious, personal spiritual relationship with God. Then, we will have at our disposal God's Wisdom, Honor, and Hope. God's knowledge, ethic, and inspiration are more powerful than ours. With the Spirit of God inside us, our inner spiritual strength is magnified many times over, being supernatural in origin and effect.

When you are faced with the death of a loved one, financial disaster, or health problems, where do you turn? A relationship with the supreme One can give us the strength that we need to overcome any situation. God can be our refuge and fortress, who gives us access to His vast reservoir of strength, His comfort, and the peace that passeth all understanding.

Nugget of Hope

The strength we need to face and conquer life's worst and best is found walking The Path of God's Wisdom, Honor, and Hope.

Far away there in the sunshine are my highest aspirations. I may not reach them, but I can look up and see their beauty, believe in them and try to follow where they lead.
—Louisa May Alcott

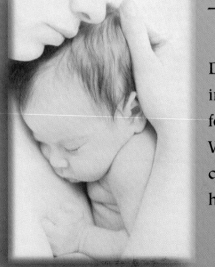

Dreams are wonderful. A mother's innermost hopes are her dreams for her children and her family. With the Hope of Wisdom at the center of our lives, our dreams have real purpose.

There are no limits to what your dreams can or should be. You create your dreams, and you are the one responsible for working toward them. You may or may not see all of them realized, and, indeed, all of those dreams may never be realized. What is important is to have dreams and always to hold on to them.

The Rev. Dr. and Mrs. Martin Luther King, Jr., dreamed that true equality among races would exist in America. You may recall Dr. King's famous words "I have a dream my four little children will one day live in a nation where they will be judged not by the color of their skin but by the content of their character. I have a dream today!" Dr. King died before his dream become reality, but Mrs. King has lived to see their dream change a nation.

One mother, with God's help, can make and fulfill dreams that make an eternity of difference.

● Nugget of Hope
What is most important about dreams?
To have them!

Change

Life can be a beautiful
journey when we open our hearts to Wisdom
and the influence of the Spirit of God. Then,
our wise hearts can
reprogram our character
and thinking.

—Cecil O. Kemp, Jr.

We have two lives.
There's the one we learn
with and the one we live
after that.

—Bernard Malamud

We don't always like change—but often it is necessary if we want to see improvement. Albert Einstein hit the proverbial nail on the head when he said, "Problems cannot be solved by the same level of thinking that created them." We resist change because we are so content with our current way of thinking, we refuse to make the effort to go to the next level.

Change requires putting forth the effort to solve problems or improve on current results.

As parents, we have great difficulty getting our children to change a particular behavior, when that behavior mirrors what they see in us. We must first be willing to change on the inside ourselves, in order for our children to mirror that positive change. We should not expect that "faking change" in ourselves will result in permanent and lasting change in our children.

Plastic surgery—a cosmetic change-isn't enough. We need a heart transplant. When we put forth the effort to make real changes inside ourselves, our children will model the outward behavior that results.

Nugget of Hope
Change which is truly valuable comes from the inside out, not the outside in.

Faith

All that I have seen teaches me to trust the Creator for all I have not seen.

—*Ralph Waldo Emerson*

Faith is the pierless bridge supporting what we see unto to the scene that we do not see.

—*Emily Dickinson*

Faith is the invisible made visible to us and others by the strength of our beliefs. Sometimes, faith is in the supernatural, not yet understood by our naturally limited faculties. Other times, faith is as easy to see as a bank check. We put our money and faith in the bank.

faith is the pierless bridge s

We have confidence the bank will honor our checks, and, when they clear, our faith is honored!

Our faith in God should be very great, since God can cover any check written on true faith.

My father says, in his book Wisdom Honor & Hope, "We understand little, if all we understand is what can be seen or explained. Truth originates and exists, in the spirit world inside and outside us, out beyond the physical or intellectually comprehensible realms of our lives."

Our children may choose roads that we feel are not in their best interest. Once we have done all we can do as mothers, then we must believe with faith that God will see them through safely. This is difficult because mothers naturally want to protect their children. But faith and worry are simply incompatible. Faith is a matter of trust in another. Worry trusts only self.

Remember that prayer is an invisible tool that can make a visible difference. Pray and stand still in faith, believing that God can and will work any situation out for good.

🌐 Nugget of Hope

Faith requires that we walk and live above our momentary circumstances, seen through our eyes and intellect.

porting what we see unto to the scene that we do not se

Preparation

Go to the ant. Consider her ways. She has no ruler or supervisor, but knows that to eat in the winter, she must gather in the summer. Consider her plans, see her manner of preparation. Follow her example.

—King Solomon

I will *prepare* and someday my chance will come.

—Abraham Lincoln

Mothers who are prepared are far more confident in the results they will achieve. The confidence that comes from being prepared reduces fear and uncertainty, in mothers and in those they influence.

On the other hand, mothers who are unwise and live by a crisis mentality, spend every moment "putting out fires" that preparation probably would have prevented. This approach causes stress and anxiety for everyone involved.

Was there ever a time when you did not study for a test? Do you remember how you felt, entering the classroom so unprepared? Most of us associate fear, anxiety, and stress with being unprepared—and fear, anxiety, and stress are contagious. Be prepared and stand clear, or suffer with the unprepared!

Humor aside, many times we approach special occasions or events in our family's or children's lives without proper preparation. It is not a matter of procrastination, but just plain lack of preparation—period. Then, we worry and experience unnecessary fear.

Careful preparation makes far more sense. It reduces fear and uncertainty, greatly increases the opportunities for success, and makes a great model for our children to learn and follow.

🔹 **Nugget** of **Hope**
Preparation is the first step in achieving excellence and lasting success.

Serenity

God, grant me the serenity to recognize the things I cannot change, the courage to change the things I can, and the wisdom to distinguish the one from the other. —Reinhold Niebuhr

The peace of God will keep your heart and mind. —St. Paul

We can face any challenge through the inner strength, courage, and peace that God gives.
—Cecil O. Kemp, Jr.

Wisdom Poise is calmness in the midst of the storms or the doldrums of life. This inner spiritual serenity is found first through harmonious relationship with God and maintained by praying and releasing matters to God, 100 percent. The peace of God will then see us through any situation, any decision, any storm, any trial.

Wisdom Poise is a calm, balanced approach to life, displayed as quiet, gracious, and humble confidence. Wisdom Poise is possible once we have confidence in God and Wisdom.

Serenity cannot be willed or intellectualized. It is knowing and believing that when we are being obedient to God's word, He always hears our prayers, and He works all things together for good. We may not always get the answers we want to our prayers, but we always get the right answers. God grants unto us peace of mind and heart while He works out His great plan.

We can have true inner peace and serenity. Just as a mother watches over her children, so God watches over us—His children. In that, we can serenely rest.

● **Nugget** of **Hope**

Inner calmness, steadiness, and peace are gifts to us from God that manifest as outward composure and serenity
—Wisdom Poise.

Success

Give me beauty in the inward soul; *may the outward and the inward be at one.*
—Socrates

Success means we do our best with what we have. Success is in the trying, not the triumph. Success is reaching for the highest that is in us, with God's great help. When you develop and use your God-given capabilities fully and in accordance with the principles of Wisdom, you achieve success as a mother or in any role. Defining and measuring success is that simple.

Teaching our children how to define and measure success the wise way is easy. Measuring Wisdom's principles and values against the spiritual and emotional state on the inside is quite simple and totally accurate. By defining and measuring success in this way, we do not create the spiritual and emotional baggage that accompany the unwise standards of modern society.

I measure my success as a mother only by Wisdom. If I develop and use, to the best of my ability and in conformance with Wisdom, the talents and skills God invested in me, and use those talents and skills to teach my children Wisdom and prove its value, living it by example before them, that is success for me.

Inner spiritual peace and contentment is Wisdom's definition and measure of a mother's success.

Nugget of Hope

Personal success should be defined by and measured against the uncomplicated, inner spiritual standards of Wisdom.

Why?

> *Man is the only one in whom the instinct of life falters long enough to enable it to ask the question "why"?*
> —Joseph Wood Krutch

> *Some people look at what is and say "why", but I look at what can be and say, "why not"?*
> —Robert F. Kennedy

Why me? Why now? Why?" When life doesn't go exactly as we would like, we want to know why. There is nothing wrong with trying to understand where something went wrong, if the objective is to correct future behavior and performance. It is unwise to get caught up with "why?" for too long, however.

There are two very distinct types of "Why?" questions. One examines the current consequence of an unwise past choice.

The other "Why?" question is asked when something occurs that is truly beyond the control we have through our power of choice. This type of "Why?" question may be asked, for example, by grief-stricken parents whose child has died. We may understand "Why" years later; just as often, we never learn the answer until we step into eternity. There is one thing we can count on: God works all things together for good for those who love Him and are living and working according to Wisdom.

While that assurance will not and should not cause us to be free of emotions like sadness or grief, we can be confident that, whatever the situation, God is in control.

Nugget of Hope
There are times in life when the "Why?" becomes irrelevant; the lesson we learn from what happens is important.

Contentment

To find contentment, enjoy your own life without comparing it with that of another.

—Condorcet

Never being content is a dangerous approach to life. It makes us susceptible to really stupid actions that are highly destructive to ourselves and those we influence, especially our children.

Many have pursued education and material possessions as priorities in life. Those are fine, as long as we do not allow ourselves to be deceived that they alone will bring contentment.

Joy comes from full use of our capabilities. When we live by the Philosophy of Wisdom and its principles of Wisdom, that's "prime time" living. Once we begin living in prime time, we reap broad benefits: joy, satisfaction, and the peace of inner contentment. Our inner and outer lives become balanced, serene, and confident.

As mothers, we are always setting examples for our children. Ask yourself: what is my source of contentment? Then look at your children and see if theirs is the same. From whom or what have they learned what it takes to be content? Is your source of contentment—and theirs—what you truly desire most?

⚉ Nugget of Hope

Being content with life means knowing God's purpose and plan for our lives, accepting these, and cheerfully and joyfully working to fulfill them.

Journey

Take me on a journey
where my heart can grow.
Meet me in the middle of the narrow road.
There's a world full of wonder we can
walk into. Take me on a journey
with You.

—Cheri Keaggy

The journey of life we mothers take
when we live Wisdom is truly a
passage from one place to another.
God leads us from the "old" to
the "new and better." The path
we follow along this journey is

Wisdom, Honor and Hope. The journey is one of faith, in the sense that we do not always know where we are headed or what tomorrow may bring.

I would much rather take a trip or a journey with the great Guide of this universe, than walk alone or dependent on my own abilities and capabilities. As Isaiah said, hundreds of years ago, "God's thoughts and ways are above ours, as far as heaven is above earth." Each of us takes this journey of life, in fear of the unknown. God will help us move beyond our fear as we walk in faith. Our Guide, Counselor, and Comforter (the Spirit of God), inside us will help us to grow and to discover wonders we never knew before.

The greatness to which we aspire as mothers can be realized on this journey called life, if we walk hand in hand with God. Then our todays and tomorrows will be certain.

Nugget of Hope
God promises to walk with us from beginning to end of life's journey; on the mountain tops, flat places, and in the valleys.

Leadership

*The residence of knowledge
is the head; of Wisdom, the heart.
A mother is the heart of leadership in a home.*

—Cecil O. Kemp, Jr.

What power a mother possesses!
Literally, when we hold and
nurture our children, we are
holding and training the future.

Mothers perform the
leadership role in the home,
especially in the eyes of our
children. It is our
responsibility, as mothers, to
lead by:

• establishing and
communicating very clearly the

the hand that ro

purpose of any given task or activity assigned our children;

- determining what the end results should be; and
- deciding and communicating how to accomplish the mission.

That is leadership, just as surely as if those functions related to a business instead of a family.

Try telling your small children to clean their rooms. Do you think they will know what to do? Instead, consider combining two leadership traits. First, set the right example. Second, be clear in your communication. Give very specific instructions to pick up all toys, put them in the toy box, place all dirty clothes in the hamper, and straighten the bed. Then, follow up to make certain the mission has been accomplished successfully. Helping them is a good idea, too. This shows them that leadership serves.

What an awesome responsibility we have, as mothers, to be the leaders of this world's future!

● **Nugget** of **Hope**
The hand that rocks the cradle rules the world.

Planning

Alice said, "Would you tell me, please, which way I ought to go from here?" The Cheshire Cat responded, "That

depends a good deal on where you want to get to." Alice replied, "I don't much care where." The Cheshire Cat responded, "Then, it does not matter which way you go. Any road will take you there!"

-Alice's Adventures in Wonderland, by Lewis Carroll

Many mothers have a strong desire to succeed, but are not sure how to achieve their objectives. If you fit that description, consider these suggestions. Write down where you are today, establish clear and written goals, and use written action plans to get you from where you are to where you want to be.

Planning applies to all aspects of our lives: spiritual, family, relationship, career, and financial. For example, most people want to succeed financially. Sound financial planning is important to achieving financial success and includes budgets for saving and spending, as well as wise investment strategies.

The desire to succeed is not enough—we must have plans and work our plans to achieve our goals! We mothers can teach our children the importance of planning by modeling wise behavior. Allow your children to see that you save money. Let them see you pay cash for consumable goods and services. Show them how careful you are by avoiding the use of credit cards and other forms of debt to empower excessive spending.

Planning is important to lasting success. As mothers, we can set responsible examples for our children so they learn to plan in all areas of daily living.

Nugget of Hope
Planning is the heart of preparation.
Failing to plan is planning to fail.

Purpose

To do good things in the world, first you must know who you are and what gives meaning in your life. —Paula P. Brownlee

Wisdom is the only compass we need for guiding our daily living and working. This compass is constantly pointing up, to remind us and inspire us that our lives have eternal purpose. —Cecil O. Kemp, Jr.

With purpose, our activities have relevance and, normally, succeed.

When our son, Justus, was born, just about everything I wanted to achieve in life changed. My purpose in living became clearer. I have been given my life, and our son's life, as gifts from God for eternal purposes.

Wisdom is my guide for living and mothering. Because God believes so strongly and passionately in the family unit, He gave us very clear instructions.

Jesus instructs that there are two ways a house can be built: on rock or on sand. The house built on rock endures through all storms; the house built on sand will be washed away. In our lives, the sand represents foolishness; the rock is The Wise Way of God. We choose which one will be our foundation.

The Wise Way of God brings God's purpose alive inside us and so it can become the passion of our lives. As George Bernard Shaw said, "This is the true joy of life; being used for a purpose recognized in yourself as a mighty one."

My husband, Chris, and I believe the most valuable lesson we can share with our son is teaching him God's purpose for his life.

Nugget of Hope

Purpose is the end we want to achieve, but it is also the starting point that determines everything we do and why everything exists.

— Paula P. Brownlee

Cooperation

I think we are here for each other.
—*Carol Burnett.*

The welfare of each is bound up in the welfare of all.
—*Helen Keller*

Almost all philosophies for personal guidance and growth teach us to compete with one another, as

the supreme personal expression of inner passion. Wisdom's perfectly excellent expression is cooperation, for the good of all.

Getting things done is a goal we all have. How we go about getting things done, however, is far more important than the actual getting done. Think of situations in which something got done, but in the end people got hurt and relationships were damaged. It happens all the time when we put ourselves before others.

As a mother, with many roles involving many different relationships, I can think of times when I needed to get something done (and I did) but in the end I felt lower than low. Why? Because I pushed, shoved, yelled, and said words in haste just so I could see things get done when and exactly how I wanted them done.

Cooperation does not operate that way! Cooperation gets the job done while it edifies and encourages others and builds and preserves vital relationships.

⬤ **Nugget** of **Hope**
Wisdom's Passion is the deep desire to serve others, not striving to win for self.

Sincerity

Be as you would seem to be.
—Thomas Fuller, M.D.

Sincerity—saying what you mean and meaning what you say—is God's way. A sincere person's inner character matches his or her reputation. Sincere people have regard for real character and integrity and do not take shortcuts up the ladder of success. Lack of sincerity will eventually lead to significant negative consequences at home and on the job.

My father shared this story about sincerity in his book *Wisdom Honor & Hope*. He hopes that his personal horror story will dissuade others from pursuing false symbols of excellence and success as he did from 1967 to 1982.

"Many years ago, I could have been arrested any day and justifiably found guilty of impersonating a husband, father, and wise family and business leader. My inner mindset and decision making model for roles and relationships were definitely not Wisdom's. My life priorities were completely jumbled. Money, business, power, and status had become my idols. I was anything but sincere. The trip was not important, only the destination. Thankfully, I do not live and work that way any longer. I now know that only the trip of sincerity down The Path of Wisdom, Honor, and Hope leads to true excellence and lasting success."

Nugget of **Hope**

We are all alike in our promises, different only in our actions.

Results

We tend to get what we expect.
—*Norman Vincent Peale*

The best is yet to be.
—*Robert Browning*

Become what you are capable of becoming.
—*Robert Lewis Stevenson*

The creative power within us can bring us abundance. When we choose to believe something good can happen, we need to have something good in heart and mind from the start.

We all want to see results from our efforts. The results that we get, more often than not, are simply the product of what we act on and expect. If we expect greatness, we will most likely get greatness. If we expect failure, we probably will make choices and take actions that lead to realizing that inner expectation.

The next time you plan any event (whether it is for your children or not), pray that God will give you the strength to see that event through, with boldness and greatness. Once you have planned, prepared, and done your part, then know God will do His part. You can expect your results to mirror your expectations—whatever you had in your heart and mind from the beginning.

We can achieve best results from our endeavors, when we begin with abundance as our inner expectation!

● Nugget of Hope
Our life shapes itself in response to our outlook, from our outpost inside.

Lewis Stevenson

Unity

All your strength is in your
union; all your danger in discord.
—Henry Wadsworth Longfellow

When we mothers create and maintain unity, the results from applying all our other personal and leadership skills seem magnified many times over. This is the impact of power united. Unity with our spouses, our children, and others in and outside our families is accomplished by focusing on the total well-being of people and on harmonious, unbroken relationships. These are the best measures of excellence and success. Our positions matter less to unity and success than our disposition toward people and relationships. Whether unity exists within our relationships, family, and other organizations is largely dependent on the disposition of those of us who lead.

A house divided against itself cannot stand. Real power is power united. Strength is found in unity, while grave danger lurks in disharmony. I believe that any mother who tries to make a house a home realizes the importance of unity with her children and among all family members. Unity is far more important than money, power, possessions, and esteem.

When a mother is predisposed to love and care for others first, then unity stands a much greater chance of prevailing. United power paves the way to harmonious relationships and lasting success.

Nugget of Hope

Real power is power united.

Thoughtfulness

Thoughtfulness

A **heart** *full of*
Wisdom

*looks beyond
selfish gain, to first*
serve others.

—*Cecil O. Kemp, Jr.*

Wisdom chooses to honor
and serve others, even if the
only reward is the personal
satisfaction of knowing you
chose to be thoughtful.

A heart full of wisdom looks bey

Some of my best memories result from the thoughtfulness of other mothers. One year, on my birthday, my friend Sasha came to the office with her two children just to wish me a happy birthday. She had been rehearsing the song *Happy Birthday To You* with Natalie (her older child). Natalie sang the song especially for me. Although their visit to see me was brief, Sasha's thoughtfulness meant so much. There was no doubt in my mind that she cared very much for me and for our friendship. She proved that she cared by planning something very special and then driving twenty-five miles out of her way to carry out her plan.

Thoughtfulness like Sasha's is the result of a heart full of Wisdom, Honor, and Hope.

she cared very much for me...

Nugget of Hope

Wisdom inside teaches that love serves others and is not selfish or self-serving.

wisdom

Blessed is the person who finds wisdom, who gains understanding. Wisdom is more profitable than silver and yields better returns than gold. She is more precious than rubies and nothing you desire can compare with her. Long life is in her right hand, and in her left hand are riches and honor.

—King Solomon

To wisdom belongs apprehension of eternal things; to knowledge, the rational knowledge of temporary things.

—St. Augustine

Wisdom can be viewed as the process of sound judgment, the discernment by which alternatives are skillfully judged, to reach the best conclusion of choice and action. Perhaps the most practical definition of wisdom is knowing and understanding whether or not to do something, and if so, what to do, and the best way and time to do it.

As a mother, I constantly seek wisdom in every decision and every situation I am faced with regarding my family. I desire great results for my family, but I have learned that I cannot get those results by doing things the same old way. Instead, I must think with my heart, not my mind. We are taught the opposite in the formal education system and most other learning venues. When I lived and worked according to their values, I was left spiritually void and emotionally empty.

So, when I say and pray "Lord give me Wisdom," I mean it. Those are heartfelt words.

People who seek and live Wisdom's ways find enormous power and fullness of joy. Remember, the control room of every life is the heart, and there lives Wisdom and its ways.

🌐 **Nugget** of **Hope**

Wisdom is highest know-how and understanding.
Wisdom lives in our hearts, not our minds.

Attitude

It is not the circumstance but our attitudes toward our circumstances that shape the types of women we have become and will become.
—*Anonymous*

The great quality of attitude is that we can choose the one we will have, in any circumstance. We can choose to approach a situation with a sour, unwise attitude that usually guarantees an equally unpleasant outcome. Or we can choose to approach the same situation with a wise attitude of pleasantness and understanding. Normally, that attitude helps ensure a better outcome.

Attitudes truly reflect and reveal our hearts. Our words, actions, and inactions reveal our attitudes. Being manipulative, for example, can be a real pitfall for mothers, if we are not careful.

A manipulative mother views people, including her own flesh and blood, as objects. This mother has a driving need to control that manifests itself in compulsive behavior. A manipulative mother unwisely uses her knowledge, power, or position to try to limit her children's freedom and uniqueness. Even the most well-intentioned mother can slip into this attitude, which is emotionally and spiritually very destructive.

Clearly, we need to guard our mindset (attitudes) and to see our children, and others, through the inner spiritual lens of Wisdom, Honor, and Hope. Then, in every situation and relationship, our unconditional love will support and release others.

Nugget of Hope
Our attitude in any given circumstance or situation demonstrates who we are and all we aspire to be in our hearts.

Commitment

The need for devotion to something outside ourselves is even more profound than the need for companionship. If we are not to go to pieces or wither away, we all must have some purpose in life; for no one can live for themselves alone.

—Ross Paramenter

Many of us are searching for the inner spiritual path home to our creator God. The cornerstone of that path is Wisdom, and the bedrock is Honor and Hope. To travel that road requires a commitment of our life and its energies. Our soul's journey is one that continues after death, though our physical body returns to dust.

Being committed means 100 percent dedication, with nothing held back. Good commitment is based on truth. Truth refers to highest reality. Unfortunately, many of us commit our lives to philosophies that have no eternal worth.

When we enter a personal, spiritual relationship commitment with God, we base our lives on highest truth—Wisdom. Our purpose becomes one that will yield lasting benefits in our lives and the lives of those we influence. We have a duty to raise our children to revere and respect God. We thus greatly improve the odds that they, too, will joyfully and willingly choose to live according to Wisdom.

Who and what we commit our lives to is the most serious of all the decisions we face in our role as parents. Our commitments determine our personal destiny and greatly influence the destinies of our children.

Nugget of Hope

We are wise when we commit our lives to pursuit of the durable and lasting, in this lifetime and on into eternity.

Confidence

No one can make you *feel inferior* without **your consent.**

—*Eleanor Roosevelt*

We would all do well to remember Mrs. Roosevelt's words.

Sometimes, we or our children may encounter a person who is "looking down" on us for some reason. In a situation such as this, the manner in which we or our children allow that person's unwise way of thinking and unfortunate attitude to affect us will either make us or break us. If we or our children permit the attitudes of others to control our confidence, we immediately put ourselves into the "fear of mistakes" mindset that cannot lead to excellence and lasting success.

Confidence arises from inside ourselves, not from the approval of other people. When our children come to us because they do not "feel good enough" to be in the presence of a particular person or because they feel inferior to someone else, let us consider reminding them of Mrs. Roosevelt's wise words.

Find your beginning point inside! You can be confident depending on what is inside, when you have Wisdom's inner spiritual peace.

Nugget of Hope

Confidence comes from the inside—from your heart. Depend on what is inside you, not what is outside.

Excellence

Going far beyond the call of duty, doing more than others expect—this is what excellence is all about. And it comes from striving, maintaining the highest standards, looking after the small detail, and going the extra mile. Excellence means caring—it means making a special effort to do more.

—Unknown

The principles and values of Wisdom set forth the best way for

doing everything. They point us to the wise and honorable way to achieve excellence and truly lasting success. Wisdom is the standard for guiding and directing our daily living and working. It is the only compass we need. Why are those my beliefs? God's thoughts and knowledge are above ours, as heaven is far above earth.
—Cecil O. Kemp, Jr.

There is a way to pursue and attain excellence with distinction. Significant success can be attained through embracing and following The Philosophy of Wisdom. Our priority then is serving others, rather than selfishly serving only our interests. The cornerstone of this philosophy is Wisdom, and its bedrock is Honor and Hope.

Mother Teresa was the modern world's best example of this kind of success. She achieved excellence by caring. Mother Teresa, the "wonder one," lived and worked in Calcutta. She made serving others her life and career purpose. As a human being, she had a choice of embracing Wisdom or folly as a philosophy for everyday living and working. She chose Wisdom—and the rest is history. What a story of success! She set an example for all mothers. Her seeds of love, grace, and generosity led to the largest harvest of compassion seen in our world in hundreds of years. She said she was called to serve The King of The Universe, and serve she did!

We all should embrace the Wisdom, Honor, and Hope of Mother Teresa. Think of what a difference these can make in our own families, especially in the lives of our children.

Nugget of Hope

The highest summit of achievement and excellence should be in our relationships, especially those within our family and career environments.

Promises

Let your yes **mean yes,** *and your no* **mean no.**
—*St. Paul*

The principles and values of Wisdom teach us this absolute: always keep a promise. That is true for any promise, regardless of its size.

Honor is important to God. One of the saddest commentaries on our society is that the ethical norm has become compromise, rather than Honor. Compromise justifies breaking promises. Compromise at home and work explains why responsibility and accountability are missing in the lives of people and institutions. We must realize compromise is a personal choice, not an institutional issue. Our children learn either Honor or compromise as their inner primary model from us parents. Our examples as mothers should prove that a promise must be kept. Honor requires that we mean what we say, say what we mean, and then do both.

For example, when two people join in marriage, they make promises (vows) to each other. The principles of Wisdom embody the expectation that these promises will be kept faithfully by both parties and the marriage contract be breakable only in very limited, specific circumstances. One of the best examples we can give our children of Honor is living Wisdom in our marriages.

Keeping our word is what makes a promise valuable. Honor is the inner spiritual ethical model worthy for mothers to emulate in our personal examples to our children.

Nugget of Hope
Our word is our bond. Keeping our promises is what Honor means.

Courage

When you get into a tight place, and everything goes against you, 'til it seems as though you could not hold on a moment longer, never give up then—for that is just the place and time that the tide will turn.

—Harriet Beecher Stowe

To lead a crowd, one must have courage to turn his back on the crowd.

—Cecil O. Kemp, Jr.

Courage is a grace that everyone needs to survive in the real world. It can be described as mental or moral strength to persevere and to withstand danger, fear, difficulty, opposition, and hardship. There are times in our lives when it takes courage just to survive.

A woman I know learned she was pregnant with her third child. Her doctors told her that neither the baby nor she would survive the pregnancy and encouraged her to have an abortion.

This mother and wife loved her family beyond measure and wanted to watch her other two children grow up, yet she could not imagine destroying the life of her unborn child. She chose not to have the abortion. She needed courage not only to make that decision, but also to stand firm in her beliefs. She has not yet had the baby, so I cannot tell you the outcome. I do believe that this type of courage allows us to press on, to endure, and to come out on the other side stronger and wiser.

Courage is unconditional love supremely expressed. Think of people that you know or have heard about who displayed true courage, placing others before themselves.

● Nugget of Hope
Courage guards the soul. The courage to act or refuse to act distinguishes the truly courageous.

on a moment longer, never give up

Honor

Character is who we really are, inside.
Reputation is what we appear to be, to others.
—Cecil O. Kemp, Jr.

We must not set our aspirations, goals, and priorities by what others value and find desirable. We must know where we stand and what we believe—and act accordingly. This applies in all relationships: with our spouses, children, friends, professional colleagues—with everyone and at all times.

HONOR

As mothers, we know the beauty of each individual. That beauty comes from within. I believe that most mothers want their children to be happy, and such happiness does not come from having, but rather from being. As with beauty, that kind of happiness comes from within the individual.

My dad says, "Honorable' is anything worthy of God's stamp of approval." Honor is who we really are inside and out, when we live and work by the Philosophy of Wisdom and its principles of Wisdom. Honor can also be defined as the manner of our inner spiritual lifestyle when we have attained inner spiritual peace, namely, a harmonious relationship with God, ourselves, and others.

Nugget of **Hope**
There is always the best way, the honorable way, of doing everything.

Communication

What is conceived well is expressed clearly, and the words to say it arrive with ease.
—Nicolas Boileau

"Thank you" and "we" are the most important words. "I" is the least.

—Cecil O. Kemp, Jr.

Effective communication must be linked directly to effective example. Communication comes not only in the form of words, but also actions. The most influential and effective form of communication is the manner of our personal conduct.

Ask nicely, when you make requests of your children. If your child or spouse or others are doing well, tell them so. Always let your children, spouse, and others know you appreciate them. If your kids make mistakes or fail, correct them pleasantly and move on. Parents should not expect children to be perfect, until they are!

Did you ever ask your children or spouse to help you by making a bed, and then remake the bed later in your own "perfect" way? Without ever uttering a word, we send clear messages to our children or spouse. The principles of Wisdom indicate the better and more effective communication occurs when we leave the bed as made, say, "Thank you for helping," and move on.

Take time to give others their due. We need to honor and serve our children, spouse, and others, by praising them publicly and privately, every opportunity we get. Honoring and serving others is what wise communication is all about!

Nugget of Hope

Mothers use wise communication to support their leadership and yield the best results in the lives of their children

Discretion

Judgment is not upon all occasions required, but discretion always is. —Lord Chesterfield

Using the wisdom of discretion leads us to be cautious and sensible, and to make sound and responsible decisions. Discretion keeps us from being rash in our thoughts, words, and actions.

Discretion involves thinking slowly and exploring the issues. That is especially important to us mothers because of the effect and influence we have on our children. Because I value the relationship I have with my mother, anything she says to me, encouraging or discouraging, wise or unwise, means more than if a friend or other person says it.

Remember the importance of using discretion when dealing with our children. Our actions and reactions make impressions on our children, creating in them inner spiritual, mental, and emotional footprints (landmarks) that will remain for their future guidance. Once words have been spoken or actions taken, we cannot take them back. We may have the opportunity to apologize for words thrown in anger, but we cannot take them back. Rash or angry words can remain for a long time in the thoughts and memory banks of our children.

Using the wisdom of discretion is tantamount to achieving excellence and success as a mother.

● **Nugget** of **Hope**
With "discretion wisdom," we have the power to gain the right result through purposeful planning.

Discipline

You must set the standard.

—*Charles H. Kellstadt*

My grandmother often bought, hid, and surprised her family with sweets. One day she bought an apple spice cake and hid it in the cupboard for a special occasion. Apple spice cake was my dad's favorite dessert when he was a child. He just could not resist the temptation. When my grandmother went to retrieve  the cake for a meal-ending surprise, she discovered instead a messy, telltale crime scene! My grandmother decided that her sneaky son should eat all of the remaining cake at once. This was her way of teaching him the real meaning of justice. She taught him that too much is more than enough. Getting too much of a good thing was a very valuable lesson for my dad. He says Granny's lesson has lasted him a lifetime and served him and others well.

Mothers use moments such as these to teach lessons that truly instill a sense of discipline and accountability into a child. It is not always easy to do, but it is definitely necessary. Teaching discipline and accountability to a child is not cruel or tough, but rather shows a mother's strong love for her child.

Nugget of Hope

A mother's love is wise and instills discipline in her children.

Endurance

God will not look you over for medals, degrees, or diplomas, but for scars.
—Elbert Hubbard

I will lift up my eyes to the hills of heaven, where my help comes from God.
—King David

The most important lessons most of us learn come on the stormy days we all have to weather, every now and then.

I almost lost control of my life when my Maltese, Princess, became extremely ill. For several stormy days, emotionally and spiritually, I doubted God's grace and mercy. For a short time, I was angry at God, blaming Him for Princess's illness and thinking that God did not care about her life. Then, I recalled what my mother taught me about such adverse situations: what matters to me, matters to God. And Princess mattered to me! She was my "little girl." I did not abandon my faith in God. I endured and witnessed divine intervention to heal a helpless little dog who was on the brink of death.

The way in which we handle adversity is far more important than our mere survival. Endurance often means pain, sweat, and tears. People we care about—even our own children—can throw harsh words at us in anger, and destructive behavior can harm us or those we love. Still, through faith and spirit, we can endure.

Enduring is very sensible, and its present and eternal rewards, very worthwhile.

🌑 **Nugget** of **Hope**
How you endure is what matters most, now and in eternity.

Expectation

The *future* **belongs** to those who **believe** in the beauty of their **dreams.**
—Eleanor Roosevelt

Hopelessness exists only in the heart that **thinks** hopelessly.
—Cecil O. Kemp, Jr.

If you **paint** in your mind **a picture** of bright and **happy** **expectations**, you put yourself into a condition conducive to your **goal.** —Norman Vincent Peale

Our life shapes itself in response to the outlook from our inside vantage point. We mothers should always search to find something praiseworthy and admirable in ourselves, our children, and others, regardless of situations and circumstances. We may not see eye to eye with our teenagers or we may experience incidents with our children that literally make our hearts ache with pain. But, when God is at the center of our daily living and working, we can know with certainty that good will come from these situations.

Someone once said that the stars shine brightest when the sky seems darkest. We can choose to see the darkness of the sky or the brightness of the stars. When we choose the latter, good will come, and positive growth will occur in our lives and the lives of our children.

Expect the best of life when you walk the Inner Spiritual Path of Wisdom, Honor, and Hope.

Nugget of Hope

When we have inner spiritual peace, we have the highest hopes and expectations for ourselves, our children, and our families.

Caretaker

For it is in the **giving** that we receive.
—St. Frances of Assisi

Nothing that you have **not** given
away will ever really be yours. —C. S. Lewis

How we define success is vital. Ultimately, being a success is not a matter of measuring or counting numbers and wealth. Success comes from caring for others. I don't mean baby-sitting. I mean putting others before ourselves. In today's world, our society encourages us to place a priority on "looking out for number one" instead of being a caretaker for others. But if we expect to succeed in all areas of life, we must be caretakers and put the needs of others before our own.

Imagine the faces of those you admire most. Are they caretakers? For me, the answer is a definite yes!

🌑 Nugget of Hope

People care how much we care, more than how much we know or have.

Gentleness

Fair and softly goes far.

—*Cervantes*

As mothers, we know that our children deserve calmness, gentleness, and kindness. Still, we all can think of times and situations when it was much easier to be harsh than gentle.

Sometimes I have to really struggle at feeding time with my baby son, Justus. Invariably, I have to remind myself of the importance of gentleness with him. When he fusses and whines about eating his solid food, I want to scream and give up! But I have learned that being harsh with him only makes things worse. Because he knows I am frustrated with him, he whines and fusses more. And harshness is not the example I want to set. In those whiny, fussy moments, the best and only solution is gentleness on my part. It involves patience, relaxation (physical, mental, and emotional), and lots and lots of unconditional love.

Our children are a sacred trust. When we remain true to that sacred trust, excellence and lasting success can occur in the mother/child relationship. It is my heart's desire, in all that I do for and say to my children, to come from a servant's perspective, always in gentle love. Sow justice and gentle love, reap a harvest of the same.

🌐 **N**ugget of **H**ope
Gentleness on the inside manifests outwardly as care, understanding, kindness, encouragement, and patience.

Unconditional Love

The best love is the love you give.
–From the country music song
"Grandpa Told Me So", performed by best-selling
artist Kenny Chesney

A mother shows unconditional love to her children by making them feel very special always. This special love and attention prepares our children to excel in life and to deal with life's ups and downs.

When my dad was growing up, his mother revealed her unconditional love for him by showing obvious joy during their time together. She spent hundreds of hours teaching him baseball, football, and basketball. She never complained, even after working from sunup to sundown. She practiced love so much she made it perfect. She gave the kind of love Antoine de Saint-Exupéry described when he wrote, "True love is inexhaustible: the more you give, the more you have. And, if you draw from the true fountainhead, the more water you draw, the more abundant the flow."

My dad now realizes that his mother's unconditional, never-ending love was an immeasurable gift. He was touched by an earth angel.

Remember, it is vitally important for your children to hear you say that you are proud of them! That memory may someday lift them back up from one of life's downs. Your inexhaustible supply of unconditional love will assure your children that their lives have significant meaning and purpose.

● Nugget of Hope

Unconditional love is Wisdom's motive. It gives without any thought of getting anything in return, and with no strings attached.

Simplicity

The secret to success is to do common things uncommonly well.

—John D. Rockefeller

True beauty shines through only when simplicity rules.
Simplicity does not seem to be a popular concept in the

modern world. We have programmed ourselves to think that the more out of control, elaborate, intricate, or expensive something is, the better it will be.

I have learned through my children that the very opposite is true. There is nothing more wonderful to me than sitting on an unmade bed in the mornings with my husband and our six-month-old son, just talking and playing. Princess, our Maltese, will usually be on the bed with us, too. It is a lot of fun to watch how fascinated Justus becomes with her. Very simple, but I would not give up that time for anything.

If your children are grown and have moved away from home, you probably experience great joy when they come home for even a short visit. You don't need a big party or celebration, but just to spend time together. That is simplicity.

All truth is simple. Simplicity is chief among the truths of Wisdom. Albert Einstein said, "God always does it simply." God has given us simplicity as the key to successful living.

Nugget of Hope
Keep it simple.

Goodness

I think I have discovered the **Highest Good.**
It is **Love.** *This principle stands at the
center of the cosmos.
As John says,* **"God is Love."** *He who
loves is a participant
in the being of God.
He who* **hates**
does **not** *know* **God.**
—Martin Luther King, Jr.

When I became a mother, love took on a whole new meaning for me. Any mother probably knows exactly what I mean. I can honestly say that Justus' love for me and my love for him have taught me what it really means to love unconditionally. Unconditional love accepts all people in the way that a mother accepts her child, as unique and precious, without bias or regard for their circumstance, status, or behavior. It breaks down walls and levels all playing fields, so no artificial barrier can separate us.

Unconditional love is love by choice and is not simply based on feelings or likes and dislikes. It is, therefore, kind and patient, never jealous or envious, boastful or proud, or selfish or rude. It knows no limits. This is how God loves us.

How do you love? How do you want to be loved?

Let your children and your other loved ones know that your love for them is unconditional, Godlike love.

Nugget of Hope

The soil of wisdom is goodness and motive of goodness is unconditional love.

Uniqueness

If one does not keep pace with others,
perhaps it is because they hear a different drummer.

—Henry David Thoreau

We encourage our children's uniqueness. Yet, we worry if they seem to feel, think, and do things differently.

Every mother sees her newborn child as God sees

His children, beautiful and unique. Over time, wise mothers teach their children the importance of being themselves and not conforming to others' views. In this way, we encourage and nurture a sense of specialness in our children. Wise mothers help their children to reveal their feelings and true thinking and to avoid activities that contradict their children's natural aptitudes and skills.

God creates each of us in His image, for a unique purpose. The plans that God has for one child are not going to be the same as those for another. As parents, we need to teach and guide our children by Wisdom and let them create their own molds by applying its principles and values.

Allow God's purpose for your children's life to be fulfilled by recognizing, encouraging, and nurturing uniqueness, creativity, and results, within an inner spiritual infra-structure built of Wisdom.

Nugget of Hope

Wise mothers do their best to ensure a child's uniqueness is recognized, encouraged, and nurtured.

Happiness and Priorities

It is not how much we have, but how much we enjoy, that makes happiness.
—Charles Spurgeon

Our dilemma goes deeper than shortage of time; it is basically a problem of priorities. We have left undone those things we ought to have done.
—Charles Hummel

What brings happiness to you?

Is it money, clothes, fancy cars, or power? If it is one or more of those things, then I would ask: have they brought real and lasting happiness, to you and your children? For me, the answer is emphatically, no! For most people, material possessions create huge spiritual vacuums, leaving us wanting more, or worse, feeling stone-cold empty!

Happiness that endures and lasts comes from having sound and harmonious relationships, first with God, then with our families, our children, and our friends. These fill and satisfy our inner voids, our deep passions, and the longings we all have for relationship, significance, and accomplishment.

My lasting joy and happiness come from watching my children grow, learn, and laugh. My satisfaction comes from spending time building and nurturing personal relationships with God and my family, friends, and business associates.

Nugget of Hope
Only personal relationships, based on truly enduring purpose, can satisfy and bring us true happiness.

Home
safe place

*The ache for **home** lives in all of us, the **safe** place where we can go as we are and not be questioned.* —George Ade

Eden is that old-fashioned House We dwell in every day Without suspecting our abode Until we drive away. —Emily Dickinson

As mothers, we have the responsibility to make a home for our children. There is a huge difference between a house and a home.

One is a structure built of physical materials. The other is a place built of something far stronger, more durable, and eminently more powerful: unconditional love.

The mother is the heart of the home. Your children may or may not remember the houses in which they live over their lifetime, but they will most certainly remember their home. Home is a place of safety, acceptance, love, and understanding, No one can take bricks and mortar and build a home; it takes a family with a heart of love to make a home.

I have been blessed that my parents built a home for my brother and me. I always feel comfortable there, at ease, loved, and at rest. Now, as a mother myself, I want my children to have a place they call home, where love abides and where loving parents will always accept them as they are, will always listen and understand.

Homes are built over time and have God and His unconditional love as their lasting and enduring foundation. This foundation begins in the love of a mother's heart.

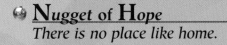

Nugget of Hope

There is no place like home.

New Year's Day
Beginnings

Look with favor upon a bold beginning.

— *Virgil*

You may have a fresh start any moment you choose.

— *Mary Pickford*

At the outset of this new year, take a moment to look back on the past year and reflect on its accomplishments. Reward yourself. Think about everything you completed successfully last year.

Now, analyze the nature of your successes. Would you categorize them as material? financial? personal? spiritual? If they were only material or financial, consider beginning this year by setting the goal of better relationships. Work this year on your inner spiritual relationship with God and on better relationships with your children, spouse, other family members, friends, and co-workers.

You might want to try these suggestions. Wake up thirty minutes earlier than usual, and use that time for prayer and devotion. Try to make certain that those living in your home sit down to eat a meal together, at the table, at least twice each week. Remind your loved ones how much you love them. Go to church with your family, at least every Sabbath day. Choose one friend to treat to lunch or dinner at least once a month. Choose one person in your workplace in whose life you will make a positive difference.

Make this year count for eternity.

Nugget of Hope

A new beginning gives us the opportunity to make our priority that which is of lasting and eternal value.

Valentine's Day
Elephant Ears & Powder Puffs

Wisdom instructs us to be long, long on listening and to listen to understand (hear). The principles of Wisdom guide us to be slow to speak, gentle and loving when we do speak.

—Cecil O. Kemp, Jr.

Words have power. Learning how to communicate with your husband or most significant loved one is essential to making this vital relationship work—and will serve as a model for your children. Success in this relationship depends on making a conscious choice to listen and being kind and gentle, always loving in your word choice, timing, and manner of expression.

Valentine's Day is a day set aside to show special attention to those you love most, especially your spouse or most significant loved one. "Love" is the key word on this day.

You have probably learned over time and through experience the importance of "powder puff" communication—being mindful and careful in all you say and do. It places listening as a priority in order to understand the other person. Wise people "powder puff" communication and listen with giant elephant ears.

On this holiday, try powder puffing your communication and listening with elephant ears. These uplift and encourage the giver and the receiver. They work a lot better than a card or a box of candy and are equally effective the other 364 days of the year. To enjoy an abundant harvest of love and appreciation, sow a year's worth of elephant ears and powder puffs.

☻ **N**ugget of **H**ope

It is wise to use our elephant ears to listen; it is wise to use powder puff words when we speak.

Memorial Day
Hope

In my Father's house are many mansions....I will come again and take you home to spend eternity in my Father's house. I am the way there. In the meantime, I will not leave you without comfort. My Spirit will I send to live inside you and be along beside you. Thereby you will have inner peace that the secular world and its promise cannot give you.

—*Jesus*

Today is a day of reflection about those who have gone before us. Those you remember today may have given their lives in defense of their nation. They may have given their lives for a cause they believed in strongly. Most important, you loved them. This day of remembrance shows us how much we need the kind of real comfort, peace, and Hope that the world cannot supply.

A harmonious, personal, spiritual relationship with God can be achieved when we accept the Hope of God. Then, a spiritual river of Hope inside us swells our dreams and hopes for our children, our families, and everyone we influence in our daily lives and work.

The Hope I am referring to also goes way beyond enhancing our present lives.

Relying on this Hope "punches our tickets" on the E-Train to our eternal home that Jesus referred to in the quotation above. This home is the one on the shores of forever, the place of sweet reunion in the sweet by-and-by with those gone before us. And this home is safe from tears, wars, and pain.

That is real Hope and assurance that tomorrow can be certain!

🌑 Nugget of Hope

As you reflect today on loved ones or admired leaders who have gone before you, know that real Hope exists.

Independence Day

Freedom

Liberty means **responsibility.**
—George Bernard Shaw

Most of this holiday is spent celebrating our freedom and independence as a nation. Have you ever thought about the freedom of choice each individual possesses? We have the freedom to choose our words, our attitudes, our beliefs, our thoughts. The one freedom nobody has is the freedom to change the consequences of our choices.

Before we exercise our freedom of choice, we should always consider the consequences. Positive freedom comes with responsibility and accountability.

We mothers, particularly, help our children learn about the responsibility that comes with the freedom to make choices.

For example, at a fairly young age, most children are allowed the freedom of choosing what they would like to order at a restaurant. Occasionally, our children choose an item that we know they do not like. We encourage them to look at other selections, but sometimes they insist on their original choice. If they don't like the meal when it arrives, they ask to order something else, but we tell them that they must eat what they ordered or not eat.

They have learned the responsibility and accountability that come with our freedoms. Freedom of choice can be wonderful—if we use it wisely. Remember, destiny is the consequence of our choices, not chance.

Nugget of Hope

We all have this powerful freedom: choice.
Exercising it responsibly is very wise.

Labor Day
Service

It's not how much you do, but how much *love* you put into doing.

—Mother Teresa

God, grant that I may not so much seek to be consoled as to console; to be understood as to understand; and to be loved as to love. —St. Augustine

The high destiny of the individual is to serve rather than to rule.

—Albert Einstein

a passion and an apt

Earnings are often the dominant factor in career choices. Some parents push their children to make career choices based solely on financial considerations. We seem to forget that money does not buy happiness. When someone makes career choices only for the purpose of maximizing earnings, that person sacrifices life satisfaction.

Encouraging your children to pursue what they truly have a passion and an aptitude for is the best way to maximize earnings. This balances earnings potential with genuine satisfaction. Because parents have such great influence on the lives of their children, it is essential that we encourage our children along those lines. One of the best ways to point our children in the wise career direction is our own example. Children need to see in their parents' lives that career success and satisfaction can be derived from pursing the passions of the heart, rather than simply being driven by financial considerations. There is no harm in repeating that money does not buy happiness.

When we pursue our passion, the probabilities are excellent that we will maximize our potential earnings. So, whatever you do, do it with passion and love. Encourage your children to do the same.

Nugget of Hope

The most important factor in career choice is serving others by pursuing work for which you truly have a passion and an aptitude.

Thanksgiving Day
Blessings

Count your many blessings.

Name them one by one.

—Christian hymn

Children are among the greatest of all blessings. Some days our children do things that may frustrate us, yet that does not erase the love we have for them and our recognition of them as blessings. So, give thanks, even on those days. Gratitude is the heart's memory.

If you have the opportunity today, as you celebrate Thanksgiving, to be with your children, or if you can reach them by telephone, thank them for all the blessings and goodness they have brought into your life. Then, thank God for the honor of being their mother.

Consider this prayer: "Thank You, Heavenly Father, for the gift of life in my children. Thank You for showing me through my children how great Your love is for me, Your child, and how wonderful heaven must be. You tell me children are a gift from You, and I thank You for a gift beyond comparison. Help me never to take them for granted and always to know that they are of You and from You."

Take time today and every day to give thanks to the One from whom all blessings come. See what God hath done!

◌ **Nugget** of **Hope**
Blessings are given by God to allow us to know just a little about the bliss of heaven.

Christmas Birth

*She will give **birth to a son**, and you are to give him the name **Jesus**, because **he will save his people** from their sins.*
—St. Matthew

The birth of Jesus to Mary and Joseph more than 2,000 years ago should be cause for joy now, as it was then. As the Bible tells us, because of Jesus' birth, his life, and his death, hope exists for an otherwise lost world.

It is easy to become caught up in the commercialism of Christmas. But wise mothers can help Christmas be less hurried and frustrating for everyone.

Begin by celebrating this day for its real meaning. Take time to sit with your family and read from the Bible the story of Jesus' birth. Let Christmas lights on trees and houses remind you that Jesus is the Light of the world. Realize that gifts around a tree are symbolic of the gifts that were brought by the Magi to the Child. Take some time to reflect on the births of your own children, and think about the joy and wonder that Mary must have felt, knowing that she was giving birth to the Savior of the world. When she kissed her baby, she kissed the face of God!

What an awe-inspiring reason to celebrate.

Nugget of Hope
What Jesus did more than 2,000 years ago is the real Hope for us and our world.

ABOUT THE PUBLISHER

The Wisdom Company (TWC) began in 1983. Its founder, Cecil O. Kemp, Jr., grew up on a small rural farm and married his childhood sweetheart, Patty. Their two children have each made the Kemps doting Grandparents. Cecil graduated college in 1971, immediately passed the CPA exam, and worked with one of the world's largest accounting firms. He became Chief Financial Officer of a publicly held stock company at 23, and its COO before 30. Since 1982, the Kemps have owned many successful businesses, including TWC.

TWC's purpose is Sharing The Hope of Wisdom. Its inspirational and character education materials all express the principles, values, and priorities of spiritual Truth—as expressed in Cecil's acclaimed book, Wisdom Honor & Hope which points to The Inner Path to True Greatness. TWC offers two series of Collectible Gift Books, The Hope Collection and The Wisdom Series. Our aim in each book is to encourage the reader and to share:

- A renaissance of the individual lifestyle shaped by Wisdom

- The way toward true excellence and lasting success

- The Inner Path of integrity in daily living, thinking and decision making

- The joy of achieving and maintaining Inner Peace, the wellspring of true happiness and satisfaction